How to be Ordinary, Mediocre, & Unsuccessful

A Humorous, Reverse Psychology Approach on a "How To" Book

by David Walters

2nd Printing 2016

Published by:
Good News Fellowship Ministries
220 Sleepy Creek Rd
Macon, GA 31210 USA

goodnews@reynoldscable.com
www.davidwaltersministry.com

Format and Cover Design by Lisa Walters Buck
lisa@lisawbuckdesign.com
www.lisawbuckdesign.com

Contents

Contents

Chapter One

"Introduction"

There are many books written on how to win; how to be rich and famous; how to become successful and how to be popular. I assume that the majority of these are written by rich, famous, successful people; or so we are led to believe. Probably a number of them are written by self publishing, self promoting individuals, or possibly scam artists, but those 'How to Become Successful' books that end up in the major bookstore chains as bestsellers are usually the genuine ones that have had successful sales.

Probably the best thing I can do to make this book unsuccessful is to make sure it has at least 300 pages. If I do that, I doubt very much if any ordinary, average, mediocre person will read it. To that kind of person it would possibly be too intimidating and challenging. So the best way to encourage the average mediocre Joe or Jane to read this work is probably to make into a short booklet. Here comes the contradiction; for everyone who wants to be or continue to be ordinary, average, mediocre and unsuccessful, they'll have to purchase this less than amazing work. If they do, I the author will unfortunately be cursed with a measure of success.

It is not beyond the realm of possibility that a vast number of successful people will be crying out for a copy of this book, especially if they are tired of all this success that they have to suffer with. Or alternatively they may want to make the book available to their students to expose them to the opposite side of the coin, which spells out the negatives or benefits of being ordinary, average and mediocre.

Because no one in their right mind would ever consider writing a book on how to become unsuccessful, don't try writing a book on how to become successful if you haven't already proved it by your own success. Although if you do write one, there are always some people that will probably purchase your work, and then they will try to do the same as you. The books on how to become successful or wealthy usually explain what you must do to succeed or mustn't do to fail.

This book is about 'How to be Ordinary, Average, Mediocre & Unsuccessful and How to Stay That Way'.

The first thing I want to say in writing a book like this; it should guarantee mediocre sales. If it becomes a best seller then in a sense, it's not worth the paper it's written on. The secret of mediocrity is not being noticed; to be lost in the crowd. Because people that are mediocre or ordinary are not unique, but very common, this kind of book was probably planned to be written before, countless times. To be sure I checked to see if there were other books available in the market on "How to Become Unsuccessful." I actually did a Google of "Unsuccessful" and found only one, sort of. I had thought of that there could have been hundreds, or even thousands of books printed, but obviously none of the authors advertised or printed a copy, so it appears that they gave up trying. That's probably why they are still mediocre and unsuccessful. If that is so, then I will have to make my book cover so compelling that non-mediocre people will feel compelled to read it or possibly even buy it just to find out how unsuccessful it is.

On the other hand as I decided to go ahead, perhaps that will make me the author a unique mediocre person that could mean that my book becomes popular and even a best seller. Imagine reading a book full of mediocrity written by a special, mediocre, unique person discovered amongst the unique. The thought of that possibility becomes mind boggling. It goes against the mediocre philosophy. To be ordinary, average and mediocre means that one doesn't want to stand out. It's considered embarrassing. One doesn't want to be a superstar or incredibly wealthy. That would be considered to be too much. Mediocre people worry over the problems and fears that follow success, for this is how they think.

> "I don't want to earn an abundance of money, because I would have to pay too much tax to the government."
> "I don't want to be a superstar, because the paparazzi would follow me everywhere."
> "I don't want to be well known, because people will dig up my hidden skeletons in the closet."
> "I don't want to become famous, because the pressure could turn me into a drug addict."
> "I don't want to be rich, because everybody would be after my money."

Unlike many poor people who are just happy to have enough food to eat and a roof over their heads and others who dream of riches, but don't want to work, and expect the government to hand out benefits to them, or they pan handle people to give them money, the ordinary, mediocre folk just want earn enough to get by and a little over for small pleasures. If they meet other ordinary, mediocre folk who want to improve themselves and become successful they usually scold them by saying, "Who do you think you are? Stop living with your head in the clouds and come down to earth. You are nothing special." If it's not actually spelled out, it is certainly implied.

So remember, to be mediocre you must follow the instructions and philosophy of the mediocre experts. Sorry I messed up. Mediocre people can never become experts otherwise they are no longer mediocre. As I attempted to write this book I found out it isn't easy in becoming mediocre and staying that way. So remember folks this is not for everyone. Many will not be able to stay the course and will either get sucked in to becoming highly successful and socialize with the elite or really poor and end up hanging out with the losers.

The Fourteen Keys to being Unsuccessful

1. One must maintain their normality and mediocrity at all costs.

2. Do not be tempted to succeed in anything of importance.

3. You must be very wary of dreams of success or greatness.

4. Always remember there is a tremendous price to pay for success.

5. If or when tempted, remember the dire consequences which could follow success.

6. You must remember who you are. So what are you? Just a nobody.

7. Take comfort, you are not alone. There are multitudes of others to support you and keep you in your place.

8. Vote Socialism. Remember the democratic government is right behind you.

9. If you begin to have grandiose thoughts, humble yourself.

10. Beware of inspiration, it could be a trick of the enemy.

11. Never, Never take risks, always play safe.

12. Never gamble or enter free sweepstakes like many poor people do. If you won you would not survive the pressure of success.

13. This is not about failure. If you don't try to achieve anything, you will never suffer the embarrassment of failure.

14. Buy extra copies of this book and give them to your friends.

Now we have established that you must learn those fourteen laws by heart and practice them until they become part of your personality. This is now your new religion. Sometimes you may tempted to travel overseas, to see other lands and other cultures; be very wary, it could be dangerous. Learn to be satisfied where you are planted. Don't go looking outside your box. Don't waste your precious time and money gallivanting to different parts of the world. There is nothing for you there. Watch your children carefully as they may want to wander off and try to do better for themselves than you have. Remind them every day that there is nothing better than what you have and what you can give them.

One of the most wonderful benefits of being mediocre is that you avoid so many bumps in the road of life that more adventurous people encounter. Most mediocre folk believe it's alright to watch a few exciting adventurous movies from time to time on TV or at the movie theater, as they know that they are usually just fictitious stories. This doesn't happen in real life and certainly not to ordinary mediocre people.

How many millionaires have lost all their money, because of unnecessary risks? Better to have a safe little nest egg to keep you going that most of the ordinary mediocre folk have to just 'get by.'

Chapter Two

"Getting By"

Getting by can be a stimulating experience and not a boring lifestyle that some so called adventurous people would claim. Taking one day at a time, on a nice even keel with very little surprises constitutes a safe and happy life. Don't be sucked in to joining the rat race out there. If you live a quiet peaceful life with little or no surprises you will probably live longer than those who are not part of the mediocre community. Learn to curb your desires and frustrations for something or someone better and you will eventually accept your lot in life that has been dealt to you. In other words, grit your teeth and endure it. Ordinary, mediocre people have the sense to know that they cannot change their destiny. They accept the cards they have been dealt with a 'stiff upper lip' as the Brits say.

There are many members of the mediocre clan that dislike anyone that was born into their culture to have any real measure of success. For example, if you did what they considered to be a foolish thing like emigrating to another country and then a few years later you visited the old country with a measure of success, they would be very irked if they found out you were now better off than they.

In fact they would totally ignore your tales of success and probably you at the same time. So if success or prosperity is somehow forced upon you, never show or admit it to them. If they have the idea that you are still struggling to make it, that will keep them happy. If you try to show them you are doing well, they will definitely downgrade you.

Vision and perseverance are not a popular word with the mediocre and ordinary. If some of them study a profession they usually end up as teachers to teach others to eventually become teachers. Academicism is usually where it begins and ends. Theory cost us little, practically making it happen usually demands too much effort and risk. They have learned that talk is cheaper than action. Hence many of our Politicians are mediocre in their so called political efforts. Often they are accused of being fence sitters; more concerned in keeping their jobs than going out on a limb to bring change and to benefit society and their country. So remember some of you politicians, you may suffer some criticism or persecution for being mediocre, but just duck and keep your head down; the criticism will gradually fade and the persecution will eventually pass away.

Do not plan to enlist your children into a private school. Government sponsored schools are best for them. They will be well brainwashed (sorry educated) by their programs. Be careful that there might be some teachers (especially in the smaller country schools) who ignore some of the propaganda curriculum that the state school board approves of and bombards the children with their own materials and free thinking ideas; giving the students opportunity for debate. Average mediocre people do not want their children breaking out of the educational system that their taxes have paid for. If and when they graduate to college, hopefully they will be taught the philosophy and benefits of communism by one of the many good progressive Marxist teachers who are now flooding our public educational system.

Unless you home school, make sure you enlist your children into a school whose standards are mediocre and where all students are treated and graded the same. There are no winners or losers in our school should be their slogan. To be proud of your children will make others kids feel inferior which is not a good thing. If you discover that your child is cursed with exceptional talent, try to curb it and discourage your child in developing it. Explain to them that it will end up doing them more harm than good.

Strongly resist the bold pioneer spirit that made our country free and independent and the people self reliant. If you feel that desire rising up to break out of the mold of average and mediocrity, remember your colleagues and friends and stay faithful to your status quo. Remember pioneer work is very risky and often dangerous, it's better to be safe than sorry. Aim for a quiet uneventful life. Remember the Bible says. "Despise not the day of small things."

Statically there are probably more average people in the population of the U.S. than any other group. So let's face up to it, most people are around average. When the new season 'American Idol' show is first broadcast on T.V. The way below average contestants seem to think that they have wonderful talent and are devastated when they are eliminated in the first round. Somehow they have delusions of grandeur and even many of their friends and family tell them that their singing talent is wonderful. Numbers of them who are knocked out in the first round, complain vehemently that the Judges don't know what they are talking about and don't recognize true talent when it stares them in the face. It becomes quite laughable to see them rant and rave when they find out they don't qualify.

True committed ordinary, average, mediocre people don't have to go through that kind of embarrassment as they wouldn't dream of entering in the first place. They are not dying to become successful; as said before they are happy to accept their mediocre lot in life. People that have gifts and talent somewhat above average have a hard time trying, because whatever they do, they are not quite good enough and they never quite make it. Then the ones that have great talent always have to cope with the fear of losing it as someone that has more personality, drive, is more gifted, more talented, more beautiful, or handsome than them, will eventually appear on the scene.

True ordinary, mediocre, average people never fall for the ploy that says sacrifice, hard work, dedication, taking risks, having faith and living your dreams will bring about success. They rest in the assurance that they will never amount to very much or go very far in life. If you are one of the ordinary, average, mediocre types and have worries about the future, just be faithful to your governmental leaders they will take care of you.

If ordinary, average, mediocre folk ever make it to heaven the angels will not put them in the front or the back row, but they will be placed somewhere in the middle, so that most of them being lost in the crowd, won't be noticed.

Average, ordinary, mediocre folk should never change their religion, denomination, or party politics. Family religious and culture tradition is of paramount importance. If their ancestors were democrats (they probably were) or vice a versa they should never change their position. They should never even consider listening to what the opposing side offer, for it's sure to be wrong. In fact, as long as the government is continuing to hand out new benefits to the ordinary, average mediocre folk; then they should continue to vote for them and keep them in power; to hell with anything else. Just advise them to pray that the government won't run out of funds and bankrupt the country.

If you are an average, normal, mediocre person and are a churchgoer don't stay with a church that would stimulate you into action for missions or miracles. Remember for the average Joe the days of the Apostles, signs and wonders are over. Even if you are unfortunate enough to become involved with a church that believe in miracles, pray for the sick, and expect God do to amazing marvelous things in your life, the excitement could become too much for you.

You would probably be riding a roller coaster; experiencing great highs up in the heavenlies and then crashing back down to earth. It is better to stay at a church where nothing exceptional or supernatural happens. Keep those things locked in the Bible. Get on with your mundane, routine, life with little or no surprises.

Some of the old religious mediocre churches teach that Christians wanting or striving to succeed is prideful and thinking that God wants to bless his children and wants them to become successful in all that they do is just too good to be true. I remember my first pastor over 50 years ago saying that Christians should never draw attention to themselves by the way they dress or look. After he said that, I finally realized why he always wore dark somber clothing and went around with a grave look on his face; with the emphasis on grave. The interesting thing though, he was a brilliant intellectual, but his appearance was very average; even nondescript. Black not only appeared to be his favorite color, but everything he wore was black, except for his shirt. You could easily pass him on the street not knowing that he was a great physician that was once in line to become the queen's personal doctor, and also a close friend of the great Christian thinker and philosopher Francis Schaeffer who incidentally wore very strange 18th century style britches. So even amongst the average mediocre looking people you can find some greats if you look hard enough.

Many people that are average were raised under a Socialistic and Communist system. I traveled to Russia and Eastern Europe just after the Berlin wall had come down and Eastern European Countries were coming out from Russian domination and becoming independent. The vast majority of people at that time didn't know how to be free, think for themselves, or become entrepreneurs. They still wanted the government to take care of their needs and at first objected to this new system.

Many older folk wanted to go back to how it used to be; having the government take care of them and telling them what to do. Unfortunately for the older ones the younger generation welcomed the freedom and self reliance with open arms. What a shame that all the old mindsets of being average, mediocre, and just a face in the crowd was disappearing. The younger generation was no longer satisfied with being average and mediocre. So beware of these freedom revolutions, they could ruin the old ways that you have held on to so dearly.

During World War Two when the Jews were round up and sent to the death camps, sadly they didn't know what was going to happen to them. They thought they were taking showers instead of being gassed. A few intelligent, wealthy and informed people managed to get out of the country before it happened. They read the writing on the wall and the signs of the times. Others found out too late and didn't make it. A few brave souls took up arms and some escaped into the countryside and hid in the forests and numbers of German citizens took risks in hiding the hunted Jews. But most were either ignorant to what was happening or just looked the other way; too scared to get involved.

Hopefully today the ordinary, average mediocre person is safe from anything like that happening again or to them. But I do have to give a word of caution to the ordinary, average, mediocre, people; if it happened again or something like it, they would be the first to go like lambs lead to the slaughter. For those who are independent, bold, above average or desiring to be, they will never just swallow hook line and sinker any government propaganda promises that are fed to them. They learn never to blindly trust or give total unqualified allegiance to anyone or any cause.

Chapter Three

"Staying The Course"

To stay average, never go on protest marches unless the government is no longer taking care of you. Never take up causes or fight for causes. Leave that to others who are better qualified. Remember to keep you head down and stay out of trouble and disputes. Having strong opinions about important things is not the business of the average person. Major your opinions on trivia, you are not put on this earth to change history or make a difference. If and when you pray, always end your prayers with, "If it be thy will Oh Lord." Remember, what ever will be, will be. Even expect your children to answer your questions or commands with "Whatever!"

As you travel down the middle road of life don't pay attention to the opportunities that will pass by you on your left and on your right. Please ignore these dangerous interruptions and keep your eyes fixed and focus on going nowhere. You cannot afford to be diverted from the path that you have chosen. Some of the best average mediocre people I have met have never flown on a plane and have never ventured out of their home State.

A few bold ones I met from Georgia did confess to me that they once visited the neighboring State of Alabama. And a few others really have thought about visiting Florida, but then decided they would wait until they retired before they took that trip. Trust me, you can't be too cautious. When in doubt always play it safe.

For those of you average mediocre souls who have difficulty of being lost in the crowd and really struggle not to be noticed then you will have to avoid crowds at all cost. Don't live in or near a city or large town. Avoid that like the plague. Look for a small town, but don't live in it. Stay outside where you won't be noticed. A one stop sign village is the ideal.

If you are attracted to live near a small town, find one that has one local cemetery plus a funeral parlor; one clinic with a pediatrician, one veterinarian, one gas station, one auto repair shop, one school, three churches, one local Pizza place, one dollar store, and if the town happens to be cursed with a supermarket make sure it's a Piggly Wiggly. If your little town can provide all the essentials that you need you will never have to go anywhere else. It's better to be safe than sorry.

As far as purchasing a car, (if you aren't content with walking everywhere or just riding your bicycle) I suggest you seriously consider purchasing an electric car. As a mediocre person you obviously have little or no interest in traveling far, so the limit of 40 miles on one battery charge should suite you admirably. And of course you will be making your current President, his environmental supporters and his democratic government very happy.

Do not encourage your kids to travel to some big city to see the sights, it's not worth the risk and they won't miss anything, sorry, they won't miss nothing. Also when they marry let them stay near you, where they belong. Just to let you know and encourage you that you're not alone or unique, half of all Americans live within 50 miles of their birthplace.

Let's get back to the old days when we enjoyed the quiet life. If you can find a house that still has an outside toilet and no electric, sorry, electricity, you have found a gem. Just make sure the tin roof isn't too rusty and doesn't leak. Sorry, I now may be going a little too far for many of you average mediocre folk. I guess I'm beginning to write about 'extreme' average people. You don't have to become an ex-hippie living out in the woods, or up some mountain, owning a pair of pit bulls and hunting game for your food.

I don't want to major on this, because I know I can take something too far. I realize that one can avoid people by being disgustingly dirty, smelly, loud, obscene and violent. Some people may want to contact leprosy so they can warn people to stay away from them, but although you will, by and large, be avoided if you manifest any of those behavior problems; you will draw attention to yourself. Sooner or later some well meaning soul, or some organization, or government official will come along and try to assist you, which would defeat the whole purpose of your efforts. You could eventually find yourself locked up inside some institution.

So considering this, you definitely wouldn't be branded as average. So I have come to the conclusion that it's really impossible to be "extremely" average therefore let's concentrate on how to stay away from all extremes and just float along as part of the faceless crowd. I really do believe that the vast majority of people are average and live mediocre lives. But there are some that find it difficult to be content to stay that way and others that are frightened of losing this lifestyle; so that's why I wrote this booklet. Remember the Bible does tell us to be content with what we have or have not.

Remember if you are average and mediocre you probably will never become a leader. You will never come top of your class, (unless the whole class comes first) as some of the more progressive, average educational, schools promote. Your children will never be an honor student, unless they are unsatisfied with being average. If that happens you may have to deal with the child that has that drive to improve above the normal.

Find out what kind of teacher at school is educating your child. You don't want your child's mind to be filled with lofty thoughts and accomplishments beyond their ability. You may also need to check out your child by researching their genes. You may have to take a test with your doctor to make sure you are the biological father of the child. Hopefully you can do this without upsetting your wife or partner. It's not impossible for average people to fraternize or even become intimate with those that are above the average class.

True average mediocre people never tire of the mundane. They love it when things don't happen, where life rarely changes. They love routine and become very upset if their routine way of life is disturbed; changes in the weather tends to upset them as they would like the temperature to be constant; not too hot and not too cold. They are usually interested in finding a job that isn't more than about three miles from their home. There are some that will travel further distances if there is public transport available. The only changes they are really interested in; is a rise in pay or an increase in benefits. Most of the time, they look to others (them or those,) to make things happen for the best, or blame (others) them or those, if things deteriorate. They definitely wouldn't look to themselves to make things happen for the better, or blame themselves if things became worst.

Isn't it wonderful that we don't have to take responsibility when others are responsible for us. It's like having a mom and pop to look after you or a benevolent 'Uncle Sam' when you are in your fifties.

Chapter Four

"The Immigration Problem"

Foreigners do and will continue to visit America. The tourist trade is good for our economy. But as an average mediocre person beware of any foreigners moving into your neighborhood. Be advised; treat them with suspicion as they probably have a hidden agenda. It's better not to mix with them and if they have kids don't let your children play with them or your teenagers fraternize with their teenagers. Don't plan to be rude to them, be polite, but let them keep their distance.

Even though your ancestors were probably immigrants, it took generations for their race to be accepted. So these foreigners will need to prove themselves. In fact, it could take a couple of centuries before that happens. Remember for the average mediocre folk things move very slowly, so don't be in a hurry and take your time. It's probably better to avoid them and if they start up a business you should be very cautious in dealing with them.

You know that some of these immigrants, often illegal ones moved into large cities and set up boundaries. The younger ones formed gangs and started illegal drug businesses, protection rackets and prostitution. They marked their territories like dogs and started wars against each other as they competed for their customer's business. These people may make a lot more money than the average Joe, but their life is usually much shorter than average. They tend to kill each other off if they don't overdose first.

Living in the small out of the way places you average mediocre folk can avoid all that mayhem, but there will probably be a few marijuana farms and moon-shiners with whiskey stills hidden away somewhere in your area. You cannot be completely protected from all the woes that surround you, but you will be safer than almost everyone by being average and mediocre. It's a great way for a long life as long as you don't die of boredom.

Thinking about your ancestors; (unless you are a Native American) they must have been immigrants and they probably weren't average or mediocre, otherwise they would have stayed where they originated from, so be very cautious as you could still have some of that pioneer blood running through your veins. Hopefully that blood will now be running very slowly, or better still crawling, so you won't be tempted to jump out of your mediocrity and run off to have adventures.

A word of warning for some of you average, mediocre folk, if you feel you would like to start a small business, such as becoming a shop keeper, or owning local cafe or a fast food place, let me give you this advice. Many years ago when I lived in England most of the small shops were owned by local people. When the Asians and Indians immigrated and moved to our local towns they found low paying jobs and rented or purchased small houses and lived together, sometimes as many as twenty in one house. Parents, children, uncles, aunts, cousins, grandparents, lived together. They often worked in shifts and saved their money. In two or three years they were in a position to offer to buy the little local shops from the older locals that were close to retiring. Then instead of opening their shops from 9.00.am till 5.00.pm and closing half day Wednesday and closed on Sunday as the original owners did, they opened at 7.00.am till 11.00.am 7 days a week. Some went on to stay open 24/7.

They continued like this for several years, purchasing other shops that had been owned by locals at bargain prices, because the average local shop owner could not compete with them, unless they were willing to work all the hours that God gave them. So the immigrants became quite wealthy. Then the local average, mediocre people were upset to see these immigrants driving around in fancy Mercedes and began to complain about these foreigners taking away their businesses; so just before you are tempted to say, "I could do that," ask yourself, "Is it worth it?" Is it worth the price you have to pay, the hours you have to work and the responsibility that is put upon you? Then there's all that worry and stress you will have to go through.

For us average, mediocre people it is best not to take those risks, but just continue to complain about these filthy rich foreigners taking over our shops and neighborhoods.

Perhaps we could shop elsewhere. The difficulty is most of those small convenient stores and gas stations are now owned by Indians, Pakistanis or Asians plus a few Mexicans.

It's an interesting fact that we have so many generations of people living on welfare that were born in this country. They argue that they can't find a job or there is no opportunity offered to them or doors open to them, yet Indians, Pakistanis and Asians come to this country and in a few years of hard work and taking risks they achieve the American dream. How do we average, mediocre, folk cope with that? What is our defense or excuse? It seems we are not wired that way. These people did come from poor countries where they had to do whatever to survive, so they continued with that mindset when they came here.

Our forefathers struggle in the past doesn't apply to us today. We are not burdened with a drive to exist or to make it. As mentioned before that pioneer blood that rushed through the veins of many of our forefathers, barely trickles through the veins of the ordinary, average, mediocre person today. We can now just coast along and trust the government to take care of our needs. So don't worry and don't get frustrated, everything will work out even if you do nothing.

Our current President in on your side; he wants you to make it, but not to fall into the pit of becoming fabulously wealthy or successful. He will do all that he can to stop that from happening by implementing his great political programs. So sit back, relax and enjoy; you will be fine.

One of the wonderful things about being average and mediocre is that you can do nothing by not going anywhere. There are lots of hard working people who work their butts off for most of the year to look forward to what they call 'doing nothing' by laying in a lawn chair at a sunny beach resort in Hawaii, sipping a Piña Colada and reading a magazine or snoozing in the sun. That may be tempting to you average mediocre folk, but remember how they worked liked dogs all the year for this brief and expensive reward. You don't have to go on vacation to relax; you can take is easy all the time, because you're not fighting to keep up with the Joneses; you are fine just as you are; safe and secure in your modest little nest. And you don't have to fritter away your modest little nest egg either. As an average mediocre person you will never have to partake in the competition of "he who dies with the most toys wins." If you are really wise and careful you will have no toys to start with.

Chapter Five

"Always Stay Cool and Composed"

Always remember to maintain an even keel. Don't let your emotions carry you away. Be very cautious about being passionate; it's not for the cool, calm and collected. My friend and his wife from New Zealand stayed with us a couple of times and I liked the way he would always answer my questions.

> "How was the meal Russ?"
> "Not too bad."
> "How was the program that you watched?"
> "Not too bad."
> "How was that meeting you went to?"
> "Not too bad."
> "How was the trip you took?"
> "Not too bad."
> "How was the weather?"
> "Not too bad"
> "How is the coffee?"
> "Not too bad."
> "How's your love life?"

No! I didn't ask that, but I often wondered what his answer would have been.

I guess the philosophy is if you only expect little then you won't be disappointed. To stay an average mediocre person one must adopt that mind set. That guarantees that they will never have any real success. It may sound sad to some, but the trouble; (as I have mentioned before) is that success brings danger. It's better not to try and climb the pedestal then you can't get knocked off it. If you stay at the bottom you avoid suffering the consequences of falling. Think of all the people that struggle all their lives to climb up the corporate ladder or improve their lot only to be knocked down or devastated. The average mediocre person is immunized from all that striving and disappointment.

I used to have another friend who whenever I asked him, "How are you doing?" He would always reply, "Fair to middling." I should have seen that as a warning sign when I gave him $5,000 to invest for me on the penny stocks market. Needless to say, I lost the lot. As I write this book I think of all the 'would be' authors who paid a considerable amount of money to a vanity printer/publisher who told them that their self published book could bring them fame and fortune, but unfortunately most of their copies ended up stored in their garage, attic, or basement. I wonder where the majority of the copies of this book will end up. Well, if push comes to shove, at least you can always end up having a garage sale.

Don't strive to become extraordinary, but continue to stay normal and ordinary. Live an orderly and quiet existence; don't even think of becoming extraordinary, for if you do you will draw attention to yourself and people will flock around you. Then you will have to stay out of sight and change your appearance and cover your identity just get some peace and tranquility. It's not worth having the fame and fortune or being renowned for being a philanthropist and a blessing to others. It's better to stay ordinary, and with a slightly below average record. That way you will not cause a fuss or rumpus wherever you go or whatever you do. If you are just ordinary then your normal reaction will be to obey orders; you will be nondescript; part of the rank and file. To achieve that will take no or little effort, but some commitment to manifest it. Put yourself under someone that can tell you what and what not to do. Then you won't have to think for yourself and avoid the danger of making serious mistakes. Stay away from dreamers or people that have great or high aspirations, they could easily lead you astray.

Stay with your own class and know your own place in life. Don't attempt to go beyond your limited ability. Accept your limitations and learn to be content with your lot in life. Learn to be happy with being normal and having low to moderate expectations. Be like the land turtle don't stick your head out of your shell too far. Better to be safe than sorry. Never devise a plan for success and implement it until you reap your rewards. The effort and commitment is too much to ask of any ordinary mediocre person. Even if you made a real commitment the odds of giving up just before you reach the winning post are extremely high. So success in making it is highly stacked against you. Always prepare for disappointments, but better still don't expect good successful things to happen in your life then you won't be disappointed.

"Exceptional" is a word seldom found in the vocabulary of the ordinary, mediocre, average culture. It could raise a storm. It is almost banned without 'exception' (excuse the pun.) To be exceptional would make one stand out in the rank and file of the faceless crowds. You probably would be branded as a traitor and ostracized. Parents would fuss and complain, "My son, daughter, has gotten all these 'high-falutin' ideas and think they are better than everyone else." They would be strongly advised to come back down to earth and not make a spectacle of themselves. Those are some of the keys to avoid one from putting on airs and graces and prevent them from pretending to be above their station in life. This will enable them to achieve the goal of staying ordinary, average, mediocre and unsuccessful.

Remember that average, ordinary, mediocre, people love and prefer a routine life. Everything in life is planned. Your church service always has a program. You know what you are going to do everyday. There are no or little surprises. Your alarm is always set the same. You rarely have to change the setting as you are not catching a plane or going on a trip or planning an adventure. The only 'suddenly' you need to be ready for is a tornado or a flood so follow the local weather forecast. Apart for that it should be business as usual, so you can find yourself in a comfortable well worn rut.

Chapter Six

"Resist Easy Money Temptation"

The true Ordinary mediocre average person will never get involved in network marketing or pyramid schemes. These are designed for the gullible and the trusting. The only quick rich schemes that bring about real riches are to the initiators of the programs. Including those that are arrested or their schemes are closed down after they have illegally milked thousands of dollars off of the unsuspecting participators.

I remember when we lived in Florida meeting guys who every three months were involved in a new marketing program and would hold meetings explaining to their followers how this was now the best scheme of all. They even told me how they made money by getting in on the ground floor and signing up as many people as possible charging around $300.00 per person and then getting out before it bellied up. They would continue this circus of money making opportunities over and over again and did quite well financially. Even in the legitimate ones only a few people at the top and those of exceptional talent or who are workaholics make any real money.

These people know that usually the ordinary, average, mediocre crowd will not get involved in their schemes, so they go after the people who are dissatisfied with their lot in life and desire something more to increase their finances and better their future. This is another reason to learn to be content with what you have, or don't have, and stay within the safety of the ordinary, mediocre, average community.

The ordinary, mediocre, average persons must also beware of investment schemes that offer great almost too good to be true returns on their investments. Usually the people that offer these crooked investment schemes go after people that have a good amount of money or savings to invest. Most people think they would recognize a crook or scam artist as soon as he or she approaches them. But if that were true they would be out of business before they got off the ground. They don't wear a sign around their neck saying "I'm a crook, don't trust me." The successful ones don't look shady and shifty. Most of them dress conservatively or like a good old county boy, and claim or appear to be good moral church going person with a family and a wonderful record of being a trusted member of their community.

The people who invest with them are so hungry for big returns that caution is often flown to the wind and they don't research these people's background history. Another problem is that one is usually introduced to this money making or investment scheme by a close friend who they know and trust. What they don't ask is how does their close friend know if this person who runs the scheme is legitimate? Often their friend was approached by one of their close friends who again didn't research the company's history, but just believed their friend. And so it was repeated, because the first friend on the top of the pyramid list took the word of the right hand man of the creator of the scheme without researching his history.

Another thing that you must beware of, if you are pulled into a money making scheme that is so complicated that you don't really understand how it works, and all you know is that you are making good money, then it's probably suspect. Sooner or later it will grind to a halt or be closed down and not only will you lose your investments and time, but also any friends that you signed up for the program. That is another reason why we ordinary average mediocre people are not usually drawn into these money making schemes. We don't live life to the full. We are either perfectly content or programmed to live life at half measure which is about average. Having ambition is not on our radar screen. Usually the jobs that we work at are about making a living and not fulfilling something we love to do.

If you have a job or profession that you are passionate about, not only will you give it your best, but you will also enjoy doing it. But if you just work to make a living then it's fine to work at half measure. That is why most of the work done in Russia during the Communist Regime was inferior because the workers were just a number so they were more interested in their benefits and handouts than having in pride in their efforts or work skills.

One of the slogans of the British trade unions (I worked at the head office of one in the 50's) was, "Workers of the World Unite." Which I believe was from the communist manifesto. Individualism was frowned upon. Workers that would not toe the line were sent to 'Coventry.' (This phrase was common in industrial disputes in Britain in the mid-twentieth century. Anyone who was considered to be unsupportive of the workforce was in danger of finding that his/her workmates refused to acknowledge their existence. Co-incidentally this was centered on the highly unionized car industry and especially British Leyland, which was largely based in Coventry. That gave rise to people who had in fact lived and worked in Coventry all their life being sent there figuratively by their workmates. (From the phrase finder.)

When I had the opportunity to work an occasional Saturday night at the one of the national newspapers as a temporary union worker I was told to work at the unions acceptable speed and not to work hard as I could put the full time workers jobs into jeopardy. So it was one hour on and one hour off. Unions demanded two men for every night job as a safety measure.

Eventually the regular workers worked out with the unions that the night would be split between two men and the early shift men would receive no pay packet, but receive a double pay packet when they worked the late shift the following week. But this was not the final outcome as the shop stewards eventually set up the ideal system.

One man would come in and after working the full Saturday night picked up two pay packets; the following week the relief man would do the same. One night on double pay 'Bingo!' With the double pay, they made more in one night than we made in a week. So if you are tempted by a little greed, it's best to get into favor with the union's shop steward.

Chapter Seven

"Staying Under the Radar"

Have you ever noticed which people get the most attention when running in a race? It's usually the winner, the runner up and the one that comes in third. Also if you think about it, often the one that comes in last also receives some attention. So the most people that get attention are the winners and losers. The ones that come in the middle by and large are ignored. They are obviously not the best runners, but neither are they the worst. They are the average runners. They end up somewhere in the middle. They are the ones which constitute the main bulk of the race. They probably don't run to win, but only run for exercise.

The looser that comes in last and few more stragglers probably have delusions of being great runners; but not so for the ordinary, average, mediocre contestants. They never expected or intended to win. Some may have had a go for a bit of fun; others went along for the ride (sorry run.) So even though the Apostle Paul wrote in the New Testament, "those that enter a race run to win the prize," is probably not true for ordinary, average, mediocre people, but that's alright; as they never wanted or expected a prize in the first place. Ordinary people usually look and dress ordinary. They are born with average looks, average height, weight, average intelligence and abilities. Their conversation is usually ordinary and mundane. The species is very common as there are plenty of them. They make up most of the masses in the civilized countries so it costs them little effort to stay that way; they just have to be themselves. They nearly always gravitate towards others that are likewise. They are not expected to better themselves, so don't see any need to improve their looks or abilities.

The women don't have much interest in how they dress, style their hair, or present themselves to others. Some of them that have potential receive no encouragement to develop it. It is expected of them to stay in their place and not be different. They must line up with the average and become mediocre. They are expected to conform and not stand out. They must fit in, even if they feel like a square peg in a round hole. It's a very safe and undemanding existence.

There are an increasing number of ordinary people who try to break out of the ordinary by following the fashions. Many American young men now shave and tattoo their heads arms and legs: grow a mustache with sideburns (reaching where the invisible shaved hair is supposed to be) and a mini goatee beard; develop a pot belly and wear scruffy tee-shirt and jeans to look cool and different.

There are now so many of them that they have become too common and ordinary and young guys with nice hair and shaven faces and nice clothes are becoming rare, especially in the south. So to be ordinary one has two options; just be ordinary and let it continue or strive to be ordinary by copying and following the crowd. The obvious reward and accomplishment of following the instructions in this booklet is that you will be able to maintain your goal of being ordinary, average, mediocre and unsuccessful. Hopefully this will enable one to live a relatively routine stress-free life.

If you have trouble accepting this lifestyle offered to you it is recommended that you continue to practice these concepts written in this book until they become part of you. As mentioned before if you reject and rebel against these principles and take the opposite path you will be in grave danger of becoming either one or all of the following; unique, extraordinary, special, popular, famous, rich and successful.

BE CAREFUL WHAT YOU CHOOSE!

Appendix

This is something that will appear to go against all I have been trying to teach you, but I must be honest.

I was on a plane traveling from New Zealand to Australia and I was given a middle seat. I'm not partial to middle seats, but as this was an airline which I don't frequently use I had to make do. As I squeezed into the seat the following story came to me. I didn't have any paper to write on so I took a bag out of the magazine holder used for emergency sickness and scribbled on it the concept. I finished the story a few days later when I arrived back at home. If you have kids you might want to read it to them or have them read it, if they can read.

Here it is on the next few pages; many of you may find it distasteful, as it appears to contradict the middle, mediocre, philosophy that I have been promoting. But step out of your shell, be bold, dare to read and become enlightened.

I had a friend who I saw from time to time when ever I asked him how he was doing, he would always answer, "Fair to middling."

-David Walters

This is the story of Melvin Michael Middleton

Melvin didn't like his first name so he used his middle name Michael. His mother had three children and he was number two so he was the middle child.

They all lived in a middle class neighborhood. There were two entrances into their neighborhood and their house was exactly the same distance from both entrances which meant that their house was right in the middle.
They lived in the country town of Middle Wallop in England.

It was when Michael was at middle school that the family moved to Middle Marsh a small marshy place in the county of Middlesex. Their new house was situated in Middle Estates. There were seventy eight houses built on Middle Estates. There was Middle Row, Middle Deep, and Middle Vale. Each had twenty six houses.

Their house was in Middle Deep and their house was number thirteen. So you guessed right; they were deep in the middle of Middle Deep, which was in right in the middle of Middle Estates, in the middle of Middle-Marsh.

It was not a coincidence that they purchased their house in the middle of the day in the middle of the week in the middle of the month of June which was in the middle of the year.

It was a three bedroom house and Michael's bedroom was the middle one. Michael was fortunate enough to sleep in a large size bed, but he would wake up in the middle of his dreams in the middle of the night to find himself in the middle of the bed in a muddle.

"Why do I never have an end to my dreams and I always wake up in the middle of them?"

Even if he dreamt ten dreams every night he still never finished them. I guess that's why he woke up in the middle of the night in the middle of his bed in a muddle, because his dreams never ended.

When his dad reached middle age he was promoted to middle management at his job so they could afford to go overseas for vacations. Every time they flew on a plane, Michael was always given a middle seat.

Michael went to middle school and wasn't very good at his lessons. He always seem to end up being in the middle of a muddle, because he got distracted and meddled with things which were not his concern or very important. Whenever there was an argument or a fight at school, Michael was always found to be the one in the middle of it.

Michael's family were church goers, but they only went on the middle Sunday of each month. They went to a middle of the road church in Middle-Marsh. There were three Christian churches in their town.
The First Christian Church was very large. The Second Christian Church was middle size and the Third Christian Church which was quite small. You guessed it they attended the Second Christian Church so they were back in the middle again.

The services, (which included singing and the sermons) were always middle sized, not too long and not too short and not too good and not too bad.

To be honest Michael found that going to church was kind of boring and rather dreary. His family tried the Independent Primitive Church for awhile, but it wasn't any different or better. In fact it was a little worse, as they didn't even have any musical instruments and the congregation just chanted and wailed during their worship time which thankfully wasn't too long, but unfortunately wasn't too short either.

Michael wished the sermons could have been real short as listening to them made him very sleepy and he struggled to stay awake. If the sermons had been long and big instead of middle size, probably everyone would have fallen asleep, including the preacher himself.

The ministers from both churches were middle size men, not too short and not too tall or long, just like their churches and their sermons.

One day Michael went for a walk and got lost in the middle of a forest and it wasn't until the middle of the next day that he found his way back home. His older brother wanted Michael to take him to the middle of the forest to show him where he got lost, but Michael said he didn't know if he could find the middle of the forest again and also the weather forecast said it could take until the middle of the week until it was nice enough to go out walking again in the middle of the day.

When Michael reached his twelfth birthday his mother said he could invite his friends for a party. He wanted it to last until the middle of the night, but she came in at ten thirty and said it was time for everyone to go home, just as Michael was standing in the middle of the room, in the middle of showing his birthday presents to his friends.

It was in the middle of the next month; during the middle of the day that Michael began to feel tired of always being in the middle. "Everything about my life is in the middle," he said despairingly. "Things will have to change! But not until the middle of next week."

Michael began to think how he could get out of this middle curse. Because that's what he began to think it was. "It seems that I am destined to be in the middle for the rest of my life," he sighed. "There must be an answer, "Help me someone! I'm stuck in the middle and I can't get out!"

Michael began to see that his whole family was stuck in the middle. Their name was Middleton and their Dad was middle aged, working in middle management and their house was in the middle of a Marsh called Middle-Marsh in a middle class neighborhood, in the middle of Middle Estates and he seemed to be the only one who realized it.

"I guess it's because I am the one that is really in the middle. I will be leaving Middle School soon and going into High School and then on to College, so I can't stay a middle Middleton. I need to become a first Middleton."

After trying various ways of getting out of the middle rut he found himself in, he finally found an answer. But it wasn't quite yet. You will need to go to the next page to find the answer, even then it will take a little while longer than the first two lines. Remember he always had to wait for the "Middle."

It was in the middle of the next week that he woke up in the middle of the night and lying in the middle of his bed in the middle bedroom that saw his solution.

"My first name is Melvin which I hate, so I chose to use my middle name Michael and I believe that's why I have been stuck in the middle all these years."

So the next day Michael declared himself to be Melvin! It was only three days later that his Dad came home in the evening, (not in the middle of the day or night) and said he had been promoted to top management.

They then sold their old house and bought a four bedroom house in Cross Deep in Riverside. Now they were finally out of the Marsh and at the Cross Roads of a new life and opportunity.

Their new house was no longer in the middle and it didn't have a middle bedroom. Then his Mom gave birth to a baby girl named Mildred, so Michael was no longer the middle child.

They even found a new church which was not middle of the road, but on fire and on the cutting edge with a great vision for everyone including the youth and children.

When their dad took them on vacation Melvin no longer had to sit in a middle seat anymore, because they could afford to travel business or first class, so Melvin could always choose to sit in a window or isle seat.

Although Michael disliked being called Melvin he knew it was worth it. I like the name Michael better than Melvin, but the moral of this story is, learn to be content with the name your parents gave you even if it's Snikkelfitz.

There is a lot more I could tell you about the Middleton family, but I feel it right to end this story right in the middle! "Why?" you ask.

Well! If Michael had refused to be called Melvin, he may have gone on to College and in that situation he would have probably been lost in the middle of the crowd, because nobody would have noticed him.

When he was old enough to drive, instead of buying a big fancy new car, he would have bought a used mid-size or middle size car.

Then he probably would have driven it down the middle of the road and hit two cars coming from both directions and ended up in Middlesex Hospital where my wife had her first baby.

If he had lived through that accident he probably would have scars down the middle of his body and eventually would have had a mid-life crises; which is a middle life crises and ended up in the middle of skid row, where all the homeless and drug addicts hang out.

Aren't you glad he changed his name back to Melvin and we ended this story in the middle?

So remember once again the moral of this story.
Be content with your name (even if it's Bubba Bellywhopper)

And don't meddle with the middle and end up in a muddle, but aim for the stars.

If successful, this booklet could become the best worst selling booklet of all time
or
the worst best selling booklet of all time.
Take your Pick!

Other Books
by David Walters

Revelation of Amazing Truths
The Anointing & You
Living in the Holy Spirit
Living in Revival
Spirit Led Worship

Books for Children, Parents & Teachers
Amazing Miracles through the Hands of Children
Your Secret Room
Children Aflame with the Spirit
Kids in Combat
Equipping The Younger Saints

Illustrated Children's Workbooks
Being a Christian
Fact or Fantasy
The Armor of God
Children's Prayer Manual
The Fruit of the Spirit
The Gifts of the Spirit

Children's Adventure Story Books
The Book of Funtastic Adventures
The Second Book of Funtastic Adventures
The Funtastic Adventures of Inisfree
The Adventures of Tiny The Bear

David Walters has written twenty three books and many articles.

His wife Kathie also writes and has fifteen publications.

Most of their books CD's and DVD's are Christian in origin with a strong spiritual emphasis.

Many of their publications are available on Amazon, Barnes & Noble, and many on line Christian bookstores.

They are also available on their websites.

A number of their publications are as e-books and some are also available on Kindle.

For further information go to:
www.davidwaltersministry.com
www.kathiewaltersministry.com

or email:
email: goodnews@reynoldscable.com
davidmwalters@mindspring.com

Or write to
Good News Ministries
220 Sleepy Creek Rd
Macon GA 31210 USA
478-757-807